WARSAW

DESTROYED AND REBUILD

TEXT: JAROSŁAW ZIELIŃSKI
COLOR PHOTOS: RAFAŁ JABŁOŃSKI

FESTINA

Text: Jarosław Zieliński

Color photos: Rafał Jabłoński
Black and white photos: J. Bułchak s.: 29 up; Dąbrowiecki p. 43 up; A. Funkiewicz s.: 2-3, 34 up;
L. Jabrzemski s.: 23 down; Ludwik Knobloch s.: 13 up; S. Kris-Braun s.: 20 down; A. Lipka s.: 20
up; K. Pęcherski s.: 48, 56, 69, 87, 90, 88; M. Szczawik s.: 15 up; St. Rossalski s.: 19; L. Sępoliński
s.: 26 down, 27, 28 down, 29 down, 34 down, 41 up, 50-54, 64, 66, 68, 70, 72, 75, 81, 92, 93;
W. Stawny s.: 37 right.

Graphic design by: Rafał and Paweł Jabłoński

Print: Perfekt, Warsaw

The photographs in this album are from the Jabłoński Family Archives.
Telephone: +48 (22) 642-06-71; cellphone: +48 602 324 409;
website: www.fotojablonski.pl, e-mail:kontakt@fotojablonski.pl

ISBN 978-83-61511-98-4

FESTINA Publishers, tel/fax +48 (22) 842-54-53, cellphone: +48 602 324 409
e-mail: wydawnictwo@festina.org.pl, www.festina.org.pl
© Copyright FESTINA Publishers ©

WARSAW

*I*n 1944, Warsaw, a one-million-strong metropolis in the very heart of Europe and the capital of a nation of 33 million, ceased do exist. At the time of its destruction, the city boasted a more than six-century-long history,

Warsaw's Coat of arms from 1659.

Napoleon granting the Constitution to the Duchy of Warsaw. Marcello Baciarelli - 1811.

marked by moments of both glory and heroism as well as humiliation and decline. Warsaw evolved from a small provincial town into the capital of the Duchy of Masovia, only to become the capital of East-Central Europe's biggest power towards the end of the 16th century. The years that followed brought with them numerous wars, much devastation and, consequently, a gradual decline of the city's political importance. The end of the 18th century coincided with the demise of the First Polish Republic which was wiped off the map after being partitioned by three neighbouring powers. The Napoleonic era gave the city a temporary reprieve when it became the capital of the ephemeral Duchy of Warsaw. After 1815, it was the capital of a semi-autonomous Kingdom of

Warsaw. The Castle Square in 1910.

Marshal Józef Piłsudski.

Poland under the rule of the Russian tsar.

The following decades, marked by successive insurrections, saw the city's local government gradually lose its independence to a proliferating tsarist bureaucracy. It was not until the First World War and a momentary shift from Russian to German occupation that gave Warsaw a new chance to shape its own destiny.

Following the defeat of Austro-Hungary and Germany as well as the collapse of the Russian empire, in November 1918 Warsaw again became the capital of an independent state.

Marshal Józef Piłsudski's welcoming crowd in 1916 at the train station in Warsaw.

Polish-Bolshevik War of 1920.

A mere two years later, that independence had to be defended at the gates of the city against Bolshevik hordes attempting to spread their bloody revolution throughout Europe. Warsaw's peaceful development lasted a scant 19 years. During that period, a great deal was done to transform a border garrison town of occupation forces into the capital of one of Europe's more populous countries. Plans for modern traffic arteries, an underground, elegant residential quarters and housing estates were drafted. Many of these projects were completed in record time, whilst the remainder were due to be implemented in the 1940s. The exhibition "Warsaw as it will be" projected a vision of a beautiful city of the not-too-distant future.

The country's cultural centre, Warsaw concentrated its leading scholars, artists and other creative personalities. Its museums and galleries displayed Poland's most priceless works of art.

Maria Skłodowska-Curie.

Saxon Square in 1916.

It was here that the most advanced research projects were conducted, including an experimental television station. Experiments on jet engines were carried out, and the theoretical bases for radar technology were developed. Experiments in nuclear physics were conducted at the Radium Institute set up by Maria Skłodowska-Curie.

Warsaw had intended to play host to a world's fair in 1944. That was the year the city ceased to exist.

CHRONICLE OF DESTRUCTION

1 September - Warsaw experiences its first air raid. From then on it would be bombed daily until the city capitulated. Heavy aerial bombardment on 10 and 15 September included the

The bombing of Warsaw in September 1939.

The defense of Warsaw in 1939.

strafing of columns of civilian refugees fleeing the city and women working in fields.

8 September - The siege of Warsaw begins.

17 September - The Royal Castle, the Cathedral, Philharmonic Hall and many other buildings are ablaze.

25 September - A blanket aerial attack by 400 warplanes takes place, during which 562 tonnes of destructive bombs and 72 tonnes of incendiary bombs are dumped on Warsaw. There is no water to extinguish the more than 200 fires that break out. Entire streets are in

flames.

26 September - Attempts to take the city by storm are repulsed by its defenders.

28 September - Warsaw capitulates in view of the hopelessness of further resistance, the suffering of its inhabitants and shortages of defence equipment, food, ammunition and water.

1 October - Germans enter Warsaw. Twelve percent of the city's buildings lie in ruins. 2,000 Polish soldiers and 10,000 civilians are dead.

21 October - The occupiers carry out their

The capitulation of Warsaw - September 28, 1939.

Warsaw in flames and besieged in 1939.

first executions of civilians. By 1 August 1944, some 300,000 Warsaw inhabitants (not to mention the human losses suffered in the Jewish ghetto) would be killed in street executions and death camps.

4 November - Nazi Governor General Hans Frank announces the decision to destroy the Royal Castle. After thoroughly looting its interior. the Germans drill thousands of holes in its walls in which explosive charges are to be placed.

Warsaw Royal Castle in flames in 1939.

migrations of Poles expelled from Great Poland, Pomerania and Silesia, an influx of refugees fleeing Soviet occupation and the transfer of suburban Jews to the Warsaw ghetto set up in late 1939.

15 October - The north-western district, designated by the Germans as the sole area of Jewish habitation, is surrounded by a wall and cut off from the rest of the city. More than 400,000 people are crowded together in horrible conditions in a four square kilometre area. By 1942, some 100,000 die of starvation and disease.

1940

6 February - German town-planners present Hitler with a plan to transform Warsaw into a "New German Town" of a mere 100,000 German colonists and several hundred thousand Polish slaves, grouped in a labour camp on the right bank of the Vistula. All historic districts are to be razed with the exception of the Old Town core, acknowledged as "typically German".

At that time Warsaw hand a population of 1.5 million. That increase was accounted for by

Warsaw ghetto wall under construction in 1940.

Jewish policemen in the ghetto in 1941.

⊰ 1941 ⊱

23 June - The first Soviet air raid against Warsaw takes place following Germany's attack on the USSR; there are civilian casualties. The next bombardment on 13 November destroys several buildings and kills about 50 people.

⊰ 1942 ⊱

22 July - The planned extermination of the Jewish population begins; by 12 September

Armband vendor in the Ghetto, 1940.

310,322 men, women and children are sent to death camps and gassed. Some 6,000 elderly and infirm Jews unfit to travel are murdered

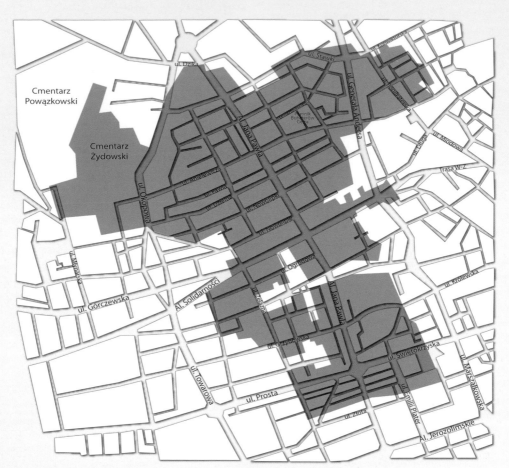

Plan of the Ghetto from November 1940 to October 1941.

right in the street. About 70,000 Jews, employed in German factories, remain in the ghetto.

20 August - A heavy Soviet air raid takes place and is repeated on 1 September. As a result of both bombardments, whose target was

Himler's order of 16 January 1943 to destroy the Ghetto.

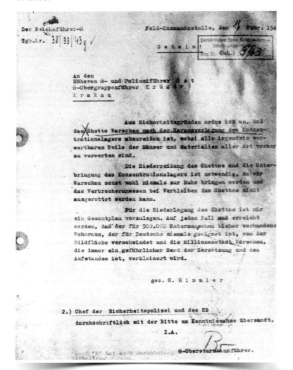

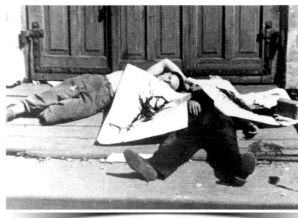

The Ghetto. Bodies of murdered Jews. April 1943.

the Warsaw rail junction, 239 people are killed and 511 wounded, mainly among the working class of the Wola district. This causes many to flee the city. German military losses are negligible.

1943

19 April — An attempt to completely liquidate the Jewish quarter sparks off an uprising in the ghetto. An uneven battle rages until 16

P. 16-17. Jews led from Ghetto.

Captured Jews during the ghetto uprising.

May. After murdering the remaining survivors, the German set fire to the ghetto then blow it up and level it with the ground. Over the next year, a concentration camp is operated on the rubble of the former ghetto, and mass executions of Poles take place.

12 May - A Soviet air raid takes place. The city centre and the Ochota district sustain the most damage; 149 civilians are killed and 223 injured. This attempt to paralyse German troop transports through the city fails once again.

16 May - The Germans blow up the Great Synagogue. General Stroop reports to Hitler: "Warsaw's Jewish district has ceased to exist."

1944

1 August - An uprising breaks out in Warsaw. Undermanned Polish detachments take over most of the city, unfortunately with the exception of its bridges, airports and communications centres, effectively defended by the Germans. Heinrich Himmler orders all the city's inhabitants killed and the city levelled to the ground.

August - The Wola district is "pacified"; within a few days 40,000 of its inhabitants are shot residents fall victim by the notorious RONA units of Russian mercenaries, known for their bestiality. In other parts of the city, units com-

Young insurgents in Warsaw.

Uprising soldiers „Rybak" aged 18 and „Kajtek" aged 13.

Town rages, ending in its total destruction. An attempt by a strong Polish force to make their way from Kampinos Forest (north of the city) to Old Town ends in bloody defeat.

September - The Germans occupy Old Town, after it is evacuated by the freedom-fighters, and murder seriously injured soldiers and civilians found in hospitals.

14 September - The Soviet army and a Polish infantry division under its command capture right-bank Warsaw. The reason for the Russian's subsequent passivity is the convenience of having the main centre of the Polish freedom struggle destroyed by German hands. An attempt by Polish army sub-units, uncoordinated with the Soviet command, to come to the aid of the insurgents cannot change the course of events, despite sporadic local successes.

From 24 September a German offensive in Mokotów district rages, and from the 28th Żoliborz is under siege. The city centre is systematically pounded by hundreds of bombs and the heaviest artillery shells.

2 October - Warsaw capitulates after 63 days of struggle. The losses amount to 15,000 soldiers and more than 150,000 civilians killed;

posed of Ukrainian and Kalmuk collaborators and companies comprising common criminals "fight" against civilians. In terms of cruelty, they are a match for the crack German police and SS units. From mid-August a pitched battle for Old

Uprising soldiers coming out of the sewers.

November/December - The city's planned destruction is carried out. After being carefully numbered, buildings are blown up by the Germans in their order of importance to Polish culture. This applies in particular to valuable historical monuments indicated by German art historians: the Royal Castle, palaces and churches. The same criteria are used in destroying museum, library and archive collections. A portion of the cultural treasures are rescued by Polish scholars. Entire streets of buildings, such as blocks of flats, which the Germans consider less valuable, are set on fire. They also system-

The Warsaw Uprising. A soldier in battle.

most of the buildings in left-bank Warsaw have been destroyed or burnt. Over the next several weeks the surviving inhabitants are driven from the city. The occupiers plunder anything that can be taken, including furniture and clothing; and destroy what is left.

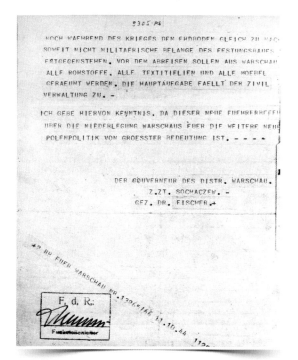

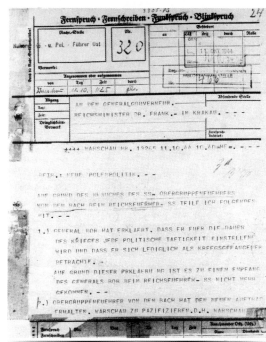

Hitler's order to level Warsaw to the ground of 11 October 1944.

atically destroy the city's infrastructure, including the power-station, waterworks, telephone lines and even trees.

❧ 1945 ❧

17 January - Soviet and Polish troops march into the area where the one-million-strong European metropolis of Warsaw once stood.

THE BALANCE OF LOSSES

*O*n 17 January 1945, Warsaw lay buried beneath 20 million cubic metres of rubble. Of the 162,000 left-bank inhabitants, only 22,000 had survived and, even then, mainly in distant fringe areas. Total population losses are estimated at 650,000 inhabitants (including some 300,000 Jews) and 200,000 newcomers (50% of them Jews). It should be noted that about 1.3 million people had lived in Warsaw when the war first broke out.

Of the 25,498 buildings existing in Warsaw

Warsaw set on fire in 1944.

Warsaw's demolition in 1944.

in 1939, 11,229 were totally destroyed, 3,879 — partially destroyed and 10,390 — lightly damaged. The last group included mainly buildings in right-bank Praga district and substandard structures in suburban areas. The destruction was not uniformly distributed. In addition to the entirely demolished ghetto, the biggest losses (close to 100%) were suffered by the city centre including Old Town. Even though

most of their buildings had suffered fire damage, the modern surrounding districts, Żoliborz, Mokotów and to some extent Ochota, could be quickly repaired thanks to their solid construction. It should be noted that in the city centre, where many more buildings had been gutted by fires than razed, older buildings with wooden roofs predominated. Only the flame-scorched shells of such buildings were left standing,

The capitulation of Warsaw in 1944.

The ruins of Nowomiejska Street.

threatening to collapse at any moment. On the other hand, most of the surviving housing displayed a technical wear level of 50%. The fate

Old Town Square, 1945.

Warsaw destroyed.

of buildings classified as historic before the war was tragic: of the 957 structures thus classified, 782 had been totally destroyed, 141 — partially destroyed, and only had survived more or less intact. Of the 31 public monuments, only nine had survived, and 90% of the municipal and state archives had been destroyed.

Also tragic was the state of the city's infrastructure. 100% of its bridges, 98.5% of its lamp-posts, 85% of its tramlines, 90% of its factories and 70% of its cable network lay in ruins. The city's overall destruction was estimated at 84%, or $2.5 billion in terms of their monetary value at that time.

An excursion of western journalists surveys the ruins of Warsaw.

1945 - In the first 24-hour period following the German withdrawal, makeshift repairs put two blown-up bridges back into service. The first inhabitants begin returning to Warsaw, some of them crossing the thick ice crust covering the River Vistula. Mine-removal operations begin immediately after the city's liberation. By 10 March nearly 100,000 mines are removed or liquidated. In February, exhumation efforts get under way. Some 25,000 bodies are found bu-

Ruins of the Old Town during winter.

Old Town Square, 1945.

ried in city streets, squares and courtyards and another 150,000 corpses are estimated beneath the rubble and in sewers.

A Capital Reconstruction Bureau is set up and begins by taking an inventory of the destruction and marking the sites of the most valuable former structures. On 11 February a wireless-station is put into operation. At the same time, the first schools reopen, and the university sets about clearing its buildings of rubble and signing up its first prospective students.

By March, Warsaw's population grows to 241,000. Its people spontaneously begin repairing damaged buildings, particularly in Żoliborz and Mokotów. In addition, a gigantic rubble-removal campaign is launched along the city's main arteries: Marszałkowska, Krakowskie Przedmieście and Nowy Świat. A trolleybus line

Podwale Street.

The ruins of Piwna and Świętojerska Streets.

is put into service, and trains begin leaving the Eastern Railway Station in the Praga district. LOT Polish Airline restore their first passenger services. The city's first restored hotel, the Polonia, awaits its first guests. The waterworks are back in service, and water again flows from Warsaw's taps.

Cleaning up the ruins of Warsaw..

Kościelna Street.

In April, the first cinema and public library reopen. The first printing-press and one turbo-generator of the power-station is put back into service. The latter makes it possible for 18 street-lamps to illuminate Praga's Targowa Street. Work is begun to prevent the further devastation of architectural monuments in the Old Town marketplace and along the Royal Way.

The Marszałkowska and Królewska Street corner.

The Saski Palace in 1946.

By May, Warsaw's population will have climbed to 366,000, and by August — 408,000. During the time, the most damaged buildings with a volume of more than 700,000 cubic metres are razed, 236 street-lamps are back in service, and the municipal gasworks are restored to 35% of their pre-war capacity. The statue of Mikołaj Kopernik (Copernicus) is the first monument restored to its pedestal. In September,

View from the cliff near the Karowa Street viaduct to the Furmańska Street.

The Staszic Palace and the St. Cross Church.

the first tram returns to the streets of left-bank Warsaw. By year's end, the city's population amounts to 467,000. Six academic institutions are functioning, 31 school and kindergarten buildings are returned to service and 11 hospitals are operating.

1946 - Two bridges are rebuilt and the Polski Theatre reopens. A mass demolition campaign encompasses buildings that could easily

The Kozia Street, view from the Trębacka street.

be rebuilt. One the reason is to salvage bricks which are running short due to the hasty removal of rubble or its reprocessing into building materials. On the other hand, the decision-makers of that day were often hostile to the urban architecture of the late 19th and early 20th century. Surviving structures of that period are dubbed "the soulless creations of capitalism" and are wantonly altered or destroyed.

1947 - Warsaw's population is now 539,000. Owners are engaged in a spontaneous reconstruction campaign of their buildings in the area of Nowy Świat, Chmielna, Bracka and Marszał-

The Church of St Anne in 1945.

kowska streets. The city's retail trade is concentrated along Marszałkowska in shops on the ground floor of flame-gutted and demolished buildings. Within these ruins are found shop interiors designed with uncommon flair by

The construction of the W-Z road.

The construction of the W-Z road.

some of the leading decorators. The street traders common in the early months following liberation are gradually disappearing.

1948 - At the start of the year, Warsaw's population is 576, 000. The building of the East-West Thoroughfare gets under way. Part of the thoroughfare leads through a tunnel, skilfully built beneath the centre of the city's historic quarter. Near the E-W Thoroughfare is built the cosy, little Mariensztat housing estate. It is reminiscent of an historic small-town square — a style unknown in pre-war Warsaw. Similar restrictions are introduced by the Capital Reconstruction Bureau along Nowy Świat, whose re-built structures may not exceed two storeys, although before the war four- and even five-storey buildings predominated. The first housing estate is built on the rubble of the former Warsaw ghetto. Because of the difficulty of removing an incredibly huge mountain of rubble from this district, new buildings are often built atop levelled earth covering what is left of the rubble-filled ground floors and cellars of

The W-Z road.

The ruins of the Ghetto. and St Augustine's Church.

The ruins of the Ghetto. in 1945.

The Ghetto wall in 1945.

the old tenements.

1949 - The population of Warsaw grows to 605,000. The East-West Thoroughfare leading onto a rebuilt and transformed bridge for vehicle traffic, is officially opened. This project is ranked among Europe's most outstanding achievements of its kind. A railway bridge is also put back into service. The King Zygmunt

The ghetto wall nowadays.

The authorities adopt a six-year plan to rebuild Warsaw. The Stalinist doctrine of socialist realism is now obligatory style in art and architecture. This is to lead to the reconstruction of the city centre into a gigantic forum of architectural innovations of exaggerated proportions and alien to the spirit of Warsaw. Although purportedly inspired by Polish national architecture, in reality socialist realism is little more than a copy of the Soviet model. The year 1950 also witnessed the destruction of the last vestiges of

Part of the ghetto wall at the corner of Międzyparkowa and Bonifraterska streets.

Column, a symbol of Warsaw, returns to its former site. Krakowskie Przedmieście is rebuilt —- now Warsaw's most beautiful street.

Having quashed all political opposition, the Communist authorities gradually set about eliminating the private sector. This involves small enterprises and retail shops — the motor force of the city's economic resurgence. After land is nationalised, tenements are taken away from their owners. Further rebuilding is to be controlled and determined by the Communist regime.

1950 - Warsaw regains the reconstructed Adam Mickiewicz Monument. By December, the city boasts 404,600 dwelling units (rooms).

Construction of Muranów over the ruins of the Ghetto.

free enterprise in Warsaw and throughout the country.

1951 - Warsaw's population stands at 815, 000. A decision by the authorities expands the city's area from 141 to 446 square kilometres. Reconstruction of the city's old architectural resources gradually gives way to the building of new housing estates: Muranów, Mirów, Koło, Mokotów and Grochów.

1952 - Warsaw's inhabitants now number 865, 000. Uprising. Constitution Square was officially opened, the first fragment of the central MDM housing estate. This showcase of the doctrine of a city "national in form and socialist

Construction of the MDM square.

Many historic buildings are hastily demolished, because their number is such that fulfilment of the plan imposed by the authorities might be jeopardised. In addition to dozens of old tenements, the victims of this campaign include such valuable historic structures as Ujazdów Castle as well as the Town Hall and Canoness Church in Theatre Square. Reconstruction of the Royal Castle is held up for two decades.

1954   Warsaw now counts 956, 000 inhabitants. The doctrine of socialist realism reigns

MDM - a procession of young people in 1952.

in substance" in reality amounted to the squalor of life under Communism concealed by palatial façades.

1953 - The city's population grows to 913,000. A major achievement is the completion if the reconstruction of the Old Town market-place. Dozens of buildings have been restored on the basis of architectural documents not destroyed in the Warsaw Uprising.

Reconstruction of Old town's remaining quarters drags on until 1962.

Construction of the Palace of Culture and Science.

supreme, and buildings reflecting that style crop up along all the city centre's major streets.

1955 - 981,000 people now live in Warsaw. The Palace of Culture and Science is completed.

This curious "gift of the Soviet nations to Warsaw" has destroyed the entire network of central Warsaw's, even necessitating the demolition of some newly-reconstructed buildings. The huge square surrounding the palace has not been built up to this day.

Construction of the Palace of Culture and Science.

tecture rings in an area of concrete, de-urbanisation and the chaotic planning and development so visible in the landscape of the city today. The following year, for the second time in its history, Warsaw would become a city of one million inhabitants...

10th Anniversary Stadium in 1955 and National Stadium built in 2012 in the same place.

The 10-Year Stadium, Poland's largest, is being built. Constructed round an artificial mountain of rubble, it becomes a kind of tomb for pre-war Warsaw. On the wave of a political "thaw", socialist realism is dying a natural death. Overzealous critics now condemn even the indisputable achievements of that doctrine — the tendency towards cohesive and concentrated development in the city centre. The first exhibition of pretabricated concrete-slab archi-

To assess the unprecedented reconstruction of a completely devastated metropolis is a difficult task which to this day evokes controversy. It is an indisputable fact that a gigantic effort was launched to restore life to a rubble-strewn wasteland. Many historical mementoes were rebuilt, partially restoring Warsaw's cultural heritage. The rebuilding of Old Town may be regarded as a project without precedent, as attested to by its inclusion on UNESCO's World Cultural Heritage list. Excellent results were also achieved in restoring Krakowskie Przedmieście, whose picturesque arrangement and the variety of its prominent structures have made it a true

Ruins of the Old Town in 1945.

Warsaw ruins in 1945.

Sigismund's Column in 1945.

sively concentrated central business district and introduce abundant greenery, the pride of today's capital inhabitants. It is unfortunate, however, that in so doing many monuments of then spurned eclectic and secessionist architecture were completely destroyed. Today, such structures are the pride of such cities as Paris, Vienna and Prague, whereas Warsaw is devoid of such buildings almost entirely. Recent years have

Nowolipki street in 1945.

gem of modern-day Warsaw. A more critical approach is warranted towards the rebuilding of the further stretch of the Royal Way, primarily Nowy Świat Street, where inordinately low structures and excessive uniformity were imposed. None of the urban palaces have been truly restored to their former splendour. To this day they await an architectural setting that would do them justice, and other important Warsaw landmarks still remain to be rebuilt. It was a wise move to "thin out" Warsaw's exces-

brought a better understanding for the art of our grandfathers' era as well as attempts to rescue surviving examples of that heritage. The process of restoring the most important historical monuments has yet to be completed.

The Royal Castle was not returned to the nation until the 1970s. Its reconstruction incorporated thousands of elements concealed from the Germans during the Second World War. The castle's reconstruction was a true achievement

Removing rubble.

Removing rubble from the Old Town Market Square in 1944.

of the art of Polish art conservation in all its aspects. The facades of the historical buildings were built on the northern side of the Teatralny Square in the second half of the 1990s and the Square was the first one to get back its almost complete pre-war look. At the same time, the introduction of modern architecture instead of the demolished buildings in the Krasiński square produced unimpressive effects.

One can only hope that Warsaw will soon regain the splendid palaces in Piłsudski Square. Its Tomb of the Unknown Solider is situated beneath what was left of the colonnade of one of those structures — the old Saxon Palace.

A more difficult task will be to eradicate the results of the inept town-planning schemes implemented after 1956. One such problem are the substandard housing estates built of pre-fabricated concrete slabs. They have not only disfigured central Warsaw but now occupy the city's most valuable real estate. The newest, typical large city buildings, most of them office towers and hotels, rarely represent innovative style any different than the average building production in Europe and worldwide. Some of these structures, usually nice and well finished, neatly fit into their space and fill the gaps in

The reconstruction of the main square.

older housing stock but quite a few high-risers seem to totally ignore their environs. The most prestigious urban planning project for the development of the desert around the Palace of Culture and Science, has been waiting years to be implemented. Meanwhile, dozens of buildings are erected at areas for which detailed local plans have not even been made. The coming years are expected to bring about significant change in this state of affairs.

After all those decades, it is difficult to ima-

Debris Segregation in 1946.

gine how pre-war Warsaw really looked. The present appearance of Old Town and New Town, including the Royal Way, can lead an uninitiated contemporary observer astray. Some of the buildings look exactly as they did before the war, some have lost much of their former splendour, while others—on the contrary—have been rebuilt in a more splendid form than ever before. Many important edifices have vanished from the city's landscape forever. Today it is difficult to distinguish between authentic and reconstructed architecture. Many buildings were built after the war in historic styles in order to provide the proper setting for individ-

Ruined Warsaw during winter.

On the construction site.

ual, valuable monuments.

Our modest publication cannot portray all the complexities of the reconstruction period. Our objective is to demonstrate to the Reader its various, different schemes by comparing photographs of characteristic sections of the city as they appeared in 1945 and at present.

p. 46-47. Old Town Square.

Old Town Square

This photograph, taken from the roof of the House at the Sign of the Negro Boy, shows the all but totally demolished Barss Side and Zakrzewski Side. In the background is seen the entrance to Jezuicka Street with the well-preserved façade of the 18th-century „Gimnasium Zaluscianum"; in the upper-right corner are seen remnants of the cathedral walls.

The reconstruction of both frontages, despite minor corrections, essentially restored their pre-war appearance.

This is all that remained of the 15th-century structure that since 1810 had housed the famous Fukier Wine-Vault.

The rebuilt façade of the building was restored to the appearance it had following an 18th-century reconstruction. The authentic ground-floor walls still display bullet-holes.

Old Town Marketplace, Fukier House

Old Town Marketplace. The corner of the Kołłątaj Side and the Dekert Side

The remnants of the corner building seen at left was once the Gothic-Renaissance House of St Anne, one of the oldest in Old Town. The townhouses on the Brass Side, dating mainly from the 16th-17th centuries, managed to escape the bombs dropped during the Warsaw Uprising but were torched by the Groans after it was quashed.

The Barczyk Townhouse and the Townhouse at the Sign of the Negro Boy, see in the photo at right, are the only ones that have partially retained their authentic 17th and 18th-century interiors.

Archcathedral Basilica of St John the Baptist and post-Jesuit Church

The cathedral, consecrated in the 14th century as a parish church, underwent many changes during its nearly 700-year history. It owed its pre-war neo-Gothic form to alterations carried out in 1837-1842 (architect Adam Idźikowski) and 1903 (architect Hugo Kuder). The manneristic Baroque Jesuit Church was built in 1609-1626.

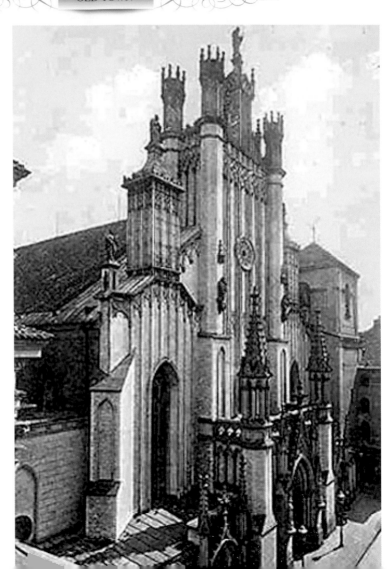

Whereas the post-Jesuit Church was essentially restored to look as it did before the war, the cathedral looks quite different. Restoring it in a mediaeval style was controversial because no accounts as to the appearance of its original façade have come down to us.

The cathedral was bombed in September 1939. Fierce fighting inside the cathedral during the Warsaw Uprising caused its further devastation. The cathedral's neo-Gothic façade and the surviving post-Jesuit Church were blown up by the Germans in December 1944.

Piwna Street

From the panorama of the burnt and demolished street, originally lined mainly by 18th-century structures. The Church of St Martin vanished entirely, having been levelled to the ground. It dates from the14th century.

During the rebuilding of this street, departures were frequently made from its pre-war appearance. In addition to authentic 200-year-old façades, one encounters some which completely differ from those existing before the war, although generally reflecting an 18th-century climate. Unlike the burgher houses, the church was painstakingly reconstructed.

King Zygmunt Column and the Royal Castle

The column bearing a statue of King Zygmunt III Vasa was erected by his son, King Władysław IV, in 1644. In January 1945, it was toppled to the ground by the Germans. Somewhat earlier, the Royal Castle, which had been gutted by fire in 1939, was blown up. The castle began as the seat of the Princes of Masovia in the 14th century, and subsequently was the royal residence and the seat of parliament. For centuries, therefore, it had symbolised Polish statehood.

The Castle's restoration was completed only several years ago, and thousands of rescued elements and fittings were incorporated in the reconstruction project. During reconstruction, the principal phases of alterations effec-ted in the 15th, 17th and 18th centuries were highlighted, and countless royal chambers and suites were meticulously restored to their former splendour.

Podwale Street and the Old Town's defensive walls

The 14th and 15th-century defensive walls encircling Old Town gradually disappeared over the years, having been densely built over with townhouses. It as not until 1937-1938 that a fragment of the old fortifications, whose remnants had been imbedded in the walls of surrounding 18th-century buildings near the Barbican, were exposed. The buildings in Podwale Street were largely destroyed in 1939 and 1944, while the conserved fragments of the old fortified walls survived nearly intact.

Since most of the houses lining Podwale Street lay in ruins, a radical move was decided to expose all the fairly-well preserved defensive walls. Where a row of townhouses had stretched along the street before the Second World War, today one can see a moat running along the old town walls.

Church of St Hyacinth

The façade and bell-tower were the only fragments of the Dominican Church in Freta Street that survived the bombardment. Several hundred wounded and sick died inside the church when it served as a field hospital during the Warsaw Uprising.

The Church of St Hyacinth was meticulously restored. It is only a shame that the neo-Gothic market stalls dating from 1820 were demolished, having been rashly acknowledged as non-historic.

New Town Marketplace

Seen here is the Baroque Church of St Casimir, erected in 1688-1692 by Tylman van Gameren as a monument to the Polish army's heroic defence of Vienna against the Turks (1683). In 1944, it housed a field hospital. One well-aimed bombed killed about 1,000 people in a single stroke.

The Eastern Frontage of the Marketplace was the only one restored to look much as it did before the war-time destruction. Unfortunately, the 17th-century Kotowski Palace, standing in back of the church, was not rebuilt. The marketplace's remaining architecture in no wise resembles its pre-war state and is dominated by early-20th-century, multi-storeyed tenements.

Krasiński Square and Długa Street

Seen in a foreground is a well built in 1823. The shell-scarred façade in the background is that of an 18th-century post-Piarist church. Next to it, at the corner of Miodowa Street, are the ruins of a monastery building and the edifice of Collegium Nobilium, a school run by the Piarist Order since 1754.

Only this side of the square was fully restored after the war. The ruins of most of the remaining frontages were demolished and the building of High Court of Justice is under the construction.

Krasiński Square

The Baroque Jan D. Krasiński palace built in the years 1683-1695 by Tylman of Gameren used to be the principal decoration of the Krasiński square. The palace and adjacent Badeni palace used to house the highest courts of law in the Second Republic of Poland until 1939. The buildings were heavily damaged in 1944.

After 1945, only the main part of the Krasiński palace was re-constructed and all that remained of the other segments and the entire Badeni palace was demolished. When the last building on the opposite side of the square was knocked down too, the square practically ceased to exist. The construction in 1989 of the monument to the 1944 Warsaw Uprising and of the new court building in 1999, brought the square and its principal historical function back to life but not all Warsaw residents are happy with the new buildings until today.

The Arsenal was re-constructed by 1950 and ten years after, the Archaeological Museum was moved to its buildings. Some improvements were introduced, mainly in the interior arrangement which now featues building styles of various phases in its history.

Royal Arsenal

The Royal Arsenal was built in the years 1638-1643 by artillery general Paweł Grodzicki. After 1832, it was used as a prison and after 1938 it housed the City Archives. The building and all its priceless archives were burnt by the Germans in 1944.

The present Silesian-Dąbrowa Bridge has a totally different appearance but rests on the solid pillars of the old Kierbedź Bridge.

The New Approach – the East-West Thoroughfare

This bridge, built by engineer Stanisław Kierbedź in 1864, was Warsaw's first modern, permanent bridge. It was blown up, together with all of Warsaw's bridges, in September 1944.

The Ghetto -- Muranów District

The Jewish quarter created by the Germans was levelled to the ground following the Ghetto Uprising of 1943. At the centre of a wasteland of rubble, ground to a pulp by numerous detonations, the Germans left St Augustine's Church in Nowolipki Street as an „Aryan" structure.

The Muranów housing district was built in the early 1950s directly on top of the levelled rubble of the former ghetto. To this day, the walls of those buildings keep cracking as the rubble ground-fill continues to settle.

Monument to the Ghetto Heroes

A monument to the Ghetto Heroes (designed by N. Rappaport and L. Suzin) was unveiled in Zamenhoffa street in 1948 with rubble heaps of flattened Jewish quarter in the monument's background.

Today's surrounding of the monument is totally different than it was before and shortly after the war, but its skyline, shaped by houses built in the 1960s, is also far from one typical of a big European capital town.

Town Hall at Teatralny Square

Warsaw's pre-war Town Hall at the Teatralny Square was built in the period 1768-1785 as a Baroque Jabłonowski palace (designed by Jakub Fontana and Dominik Merlini). It was converted into the seat of Warsaw's city authorities in 1817 and then the medieval Town Hall at the Old Town Market Square was demolished. The Building was expanded in the years 1865-1869 (construction design by Rafał Krajewski and Józef Orłowski). At that time, the building received its tall roofs, a tower, and an office annex on the left side.

The Town Hall building was re-erected in 1997 together with the other buildings along the northern side of the square. But the building's historical shapes were restored only facade-deep using concrete casts. Behind the facades are banks housed by high tech but ordinary-shaped buildings with rather utilitarian interiors. The re-construction methods and the present function of the building used to be controversial for public opinion.

The Town Hall was burnt and heavily damaged during the 1944 Warsaw Uprising but its condition was still good enough for re-construction. However, the communist rulers with their aversion to the building which they considered a symbol of independence of the Warsaw local authorities, preferred to have the ruins levelled in 1954 for whi9ch they used a pretext that when re-built, it would obscure the view from the new W-Z road on the Grand Theatre on the opposite side of the square.

Old Town panorama as seen from Krakowskie Przedmieście

A shapeless mass of ruins was all that remained of the 650-year-old Old Town complex. The walls seen at right are those of the bell-tower of St Anne's Church and a now non-existent 18th-century townhouse.

The surviving façades of the 17th and 18th-century buildings seen at left were largely demolished during construction of the E-W Thoroughfare and subsequently rather meticulously rebuilt.

Krakowskie Przedmieście

The walls of big 19th and 20th-century tenements predominated among the ruins of the 18th-century townhouses. Seen in the foreground is a townhouse built in 1884 and once belonging to the Hille & Dietrich Textile Works of Żyrardów.

After the war, all the newer tenements were either demolished or completely altered. All the surviving 19th-century façade decorations were also entirely obliterated. The entire complex was given an 18th-century appearance featuring pseudo-classical details and artificially equalised dimensions.

Most of the houses walls were successfully saved from damage during the construction of the W-Z road. The house was fully rebuilt by 1949 when the conservators restored it to the style of the second half of 18th century. It was possible owing to photo-quality paintings by Bernardo Bellotto, known as Canaletto.

The Prażmowski House

The Prażmowski house, refurbished by Jakub Fontana for the Leszczyński family, was one of the most beautiful houses in the Krakowskie Przedmieście Avenue before 1939, despite several modifications which changed its style. After 1944, the house was a burnt shell with surviving Rococo ornaments on it.

The rebuilt townhouses were made equal in height and considerably stripped of their stylistic embellishments.

Krakowskie Przedmieście.

In spite of the destruction, the pre-war street's differentiation in terms of style and dimensions can be clearly seen.

Saxon Palace - The Tomb of the Unknown Soldier

This edifice was erected towards the end of the 17th century but received its final form in 1842, when it was altered by Wacław Ritschl and Adam Idźikowski. In 1923 the Prince Józef Poniatowski monument, regained from the Russians, was placed in front of the palace's colonnade. Two years later, the Tomb of the Unknown Soldier was enshrined beneath its arcades.

That surviving fragment is today the only trace of the monumental palatial architecture that once graced Piłsudski Square. Its function has not changed. The reconstructed Prince Józef Poniatowski monument stands in Krakowskie Przedmieście.

The palace was blown up by the Germans in November 1944. By some strange coincidence, only the fragment containing the Tomb of the Unknown Soldier survived. the explosion.

Nowy Świat Street

The architectural contrasts here were even greater than those of Krakowskie Przedmieście.

The street was all but entirely destroyed in 1939 and 1944.

During the reconstruction, a height of two storeys was adopted as the norm. That meant that some buildings were shortened by all of three storeys in an attempt to restore the street's early-19th century appearance. Once a big-city street, today Nowy Świat conveys a clearly provincial image.

As a result of the principle of preserving former façades and standardising heights, most of the rowhouses were rebuilt without any major changes, but the Hotel Savoy vanished from Nowy Świat without a trace.

Nowy Świat Street

This complex of flame-gutted tenements before the war had comprised one of the few enclaves of authentic early-19th-century architecture. Seen in the background are the jutting walls of the Secession-style Hotel Savoy.

St. Alexander's Church

The shape of the classicistic St. Alexander's Church at the Three Crosses Square refers to Rome's Pantheon. Its construction, according to blueprints by Jakub Kubicki, was finished in 1825. The church was expanded and re-arranged by Józef P. Dziekoński at the end of the 19th century. It was turned into rubble by bombs thrown by German Stukas; planes in September 1944.

During the church's re-construction (1949-1950), the architects restored its shape close to the original design plus Dziekoński's lower church (in the basement) and all that remained from the interior decorations and outfit.

Ujazdów Castle

Erected as the royal residence of King Władysław IV in 1624-1637, Ujazdów Castle over the years it had undergone frequent transformations. For 130 years it had served as a military hospital. In 1944 it was burnt down to the ground by the German „Vernichtungskommando".

The castle's well-preserved walls were demolished down to their foundations on orders from the Communist military authorities in 1953. Plans were drawn up to establish a Polish Army theatre at the site, but fortunately they never materialised. The castle was restored in the 1970s to closely resemble the way it looked originally.

Poniatowski Bridge

The nicest of Warsaw's old bridges known as the Prince Józef Poniatowski Bridge was built in 1913. Its stylish appearance was designed by Stefan Szyller, one of the most prominent Warsaw architects at the time. Only two years after the construction, Russian troops fleeing from the Germans blew the bridge up. The bridge was destroyed for the second time, much more completely, by the Germans in 1944.

When the city was free again, the reconstruction of the bridge was done in such a haste that it ended in a construction catastrophe. The work was eventually finished in July 1946 but the builders gave up restoring all the architectural details on the parts which were re-built from scratch.

The former Prudential Building – today's Hotel Warszawa

Pre-war Warsaw's tallest building was completed in 1933 according to a design by Marcin Weinfeld. The skyscraper's steel construction, designed by Prof. Stefan Bryła, was so strong that it even endured a shelling by the Germans' heaviest 610-millimetre super-mortar Karl.

During post-war reconstruction, Weinfeld disfigured his creation by decorating the building with abundant socialist-realist details. Today the building serves as Hotel Warszawa.

The ruins of the PKO building had been an eye-sore until the 1960s, when they finally gave way to the East Wall building project. Both considerably widened streets bear no resemblance to their pre-war appearance.

Świętokrzyska Street.

Among the ruins of blocks of flats is seen a modern building that had been hit by a heavy bomb. Situated at the corner of Marszałkowska, it was built in 1939 by Bolesław Szmidt and belonged to the Postal Savings Bank (PKO).

Main Railway Station – City Centre Station

Designed by Czesław Przybylski and built right up to the outbreak of World War Two, it was Europe's most modern railway station of its time.

On the site of the former Main Train Station, an entrance pavilion to the City Centre Station of the electric suburban railway was built, but it is the Palace of Culture, that gigantic, grotesque memento of the Stalin era, that captures one's attention.

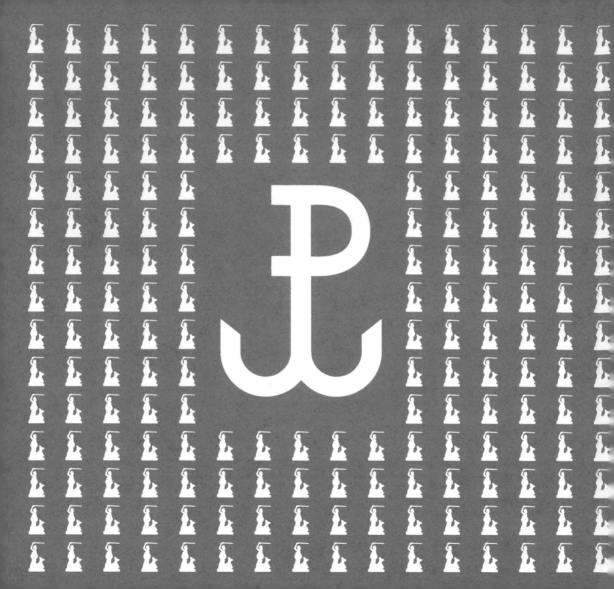